An Unbecoming Fit of Frenzy

An Unbecoming Fit of Frenzy

Bruce McRae

© 2015 by Bruce McRae

All rights reserved. No part of this publication may be reproduced, stored in a retrieval system, distributed, or transmitted in any form, or by any means, including photocopying, recording, or other electronic or mechanical methods now available or that may become available in the future without the prior written permission of the publisher.

For permission requests, email the publisher at: inquiry@cawingcrowpress.com

Published by:
Cawing Crow Press LLC
Dunlo, PA

ISBN: 978-1-68264-005-0
Library of Congress Control Number: 2015955455

Visit us on the web at: www.cawingcrowpress.com

Acknowledgements:- some of these poems have been previously published in *A Baker's Dozen, Bijou Poetry Review, The Dawn Treader, Forge, Hawai'I Pacific Review, Island Writer, Labour Of Love, Lightning'd Press, Obsession Literary Magazine. Poetic Hours, PoetryMagazine.com, Straight Forward Poetry, Symmetry Pebbles, Taj Mahal Review, Visions International, Wilderness House, and The Write Room*

to ma and pa

Introduction
by Adrew Cartmel

I first met Bruce McRae when he was living in London, England, doing the wandering-writer boho thing in the great tradition of the two Jacks — London (no relation) and Kerouac. Like Jack London he was working with his hands and getting a glimpse of this city in all its cold-water seediness. Like Jack Kerouac he was taking his experience and transforming it into language which pushes at the boundaries — not to mention being beautiful.

And insightful. And funny.

No mean trifecta.

I'm a writer too, but no practising poet (the toughest gig in literature).

While Bruce was composing verse I was busy script-editing a science fiction TV show called *Doctor Who*. While he was living in remote cabins and going toe to toe with the wilderness, inside and outside of all of us, I was worrying about dodgy monster make-up and sets which wobbled. His concerns were eternal and existential. Mine centred on cheapo special effects.

Where we overlap, though, is the wonderful word of words.

Whereas I craft dialogue and scene directions to be turned into coloured light on television sets, Bruce weaves poetry destined to be projected in the movie theatre of your mind.

And we share a concern for science and a fondness for classic science fiction. Bruce is after all the man who penned 'Space Academy' ("while we're smoking behind the launching pad./We look to the stars").

Bruce McRae blends well informed futurist, pulp fictioneer and cocky raconteur in the demotic — which is to say, he speaks fluent slang. Which is why I love his stuff: "Here's the poor sap going broke/by the deflected light of the half moon."

And more lunar observations: "the moon comes around,/like an old man looking for a slipper."

It's as good an image as has been coined since we moved into the caves and starting composing poems. And funnier than anything in Milton.

This is Bruce all over. The sly humour, the precision of his language which encompasses everything from high cosmic art to low human comedy.

He's becomingly modest ("You'd get more sense out of a talking hedge") but in fact there is no one you'd be better off getting the word from than our Bruce.

This book in your hands (or on your screen) is poetry for poetry lovers, but also poetry haters.

Even those who've shunned verse since it was briefly force-fed to them at junior school will be pleasantly surprised to flip through these pages and find how easy they are to read, how engaging and conversational and charming.

And above all, vivid, perceptive and profound.

And funny.

It's hard to imagine anyone without an operational set of eyeballs and a functioning cerebral cortex who wouldn't get something out of this collection — and if you don't have the eyes just now, you can always get someone else to read it to you. Maybe Bruce himself, online, thanks to our magical new world of the interweb.

It's a new world which calls for a new poet. One who is clear sighted enough to read the signs, quick witted and well read enough to interpret them. And talented and droll enough to tell us all about it in words we'll understand, and enjoy and treasure.

Bruce McRae is your man. Being in his company isn't just entertaining, engaging and exciting. It's educational. But don't let that put you off, kids. I'm now aware that 'vatic' means predicting the future while a 'maenad' is a female follower of Dionysus. (Any fool knows *that*.)

He's witty ("petty thieves stealing forty winks") and he's fluent in the language of science. Unusual to find a versifier who knows he's "at the bottom of this gravity-well", who is willing to stare into the compound eyes of insects, to speak of "hanging from physics' invisible wires."

Or, best yet, to magnificently describe distant stars as "the taillights of those departing."

Which brings us to Bruce's trump card, his marvellous gift for imagery.

In his verse, "A mood arrives in its torn black envelope," while "Strangers rummaged through my/ head as one would rifle in a knife drawer."

So if "Leaves rustling bring to mind applause," then I say that this chlorophyll- green applause is for Mr McRae.

He's a phrasemaker. Maybe even a phrase monger.

"My girl is a fallen angel,/her voice like a ball gown being unzipped."

In fact, he's a poet.

Andrew Cartmel
London

*Andrew Cartmel is a Canadian writer living in England. One day he may be an English writer living in Canada. He has written novels, stage plays, television scripts, song lyrics and graphic novels, but never poetry. His era as a script editor on Doctor Who is much discussed in certain quarters.

Contents

Introduction vii

Part One 1

    Eventide 3

    Of Course, This was Some Time Ago 4

    We Who Flee 5

    Getting There 6

    Trip 7

    Small Town Blues 8

    Dark and Stormy Night 9

    One Morning 10

    Dragged Out in Chains 11

    This Too Passes 12

    Haunted House 13

    Address Unknown 14

    House to House 15

    Absentee Landlord 16

    Moth to a Flame 17

    Glass and Steel 18

    Lost Ticket 19

    Out of the Way Place 20

    Gag Order 21

Part Two 23

    The Volume of Man 25

    Whatever 26

Moving Target 27
The Will of the People 28
In a Bottle 29
The Message and the Messenger 30
Black Light 31
Mortal Midnight 32
One Night Among Many 33
Falling Star 34
High Mass 35
God's Button 36
Hush 37
Your Prayers are Welcomed 38
Condemned 39
The Infinite Voice-Over of Eternal Essences 40
Unquenchable Fire 41
Deep Blue Sea 42

Part Three 43
Sonnet Despairing 45
It Is Our Nature 46
The Christmas Syndrome 47
A Long Stretch in the Slammer 48
Everlasting Pardon 49
Zip Your Lip 50
It's a Living 51
Cometh the Hour 52

Nowhere Now 53
A Solitary Mister 54
The Bee's Knees 55
Can You Spare an Emotion? 56
Chez André 57
After a Long Night 58
Charming 59
In a Burning Book 60
A Book 61
Mouthful 62
Not That Poem 63
On Paper 64
Squinting 65
Posthumous Opus 66

Part Four 67
Love Is Also a Weapon 69
Trial by Fire 70
A Seven-Headed Love Story 71
Cold Flame 72
Assigned False Planets 73
Beautiful Monster 74
The Play of Shadows 75
Mystery Play 76
First Night 77
My Life in Movies 78

Now Showing	79
The Joke's on You	81
Wolf Song	82
Bugged-Out	83
The Spider Says	84
Faint Olympian	85
Death of a Mouse	86
Under the World	87
Invention	88
Ponderous Breezes	89
N Equals N	90
Zero Point Zero	91
Here Is Now	92
About the Author	95

The Poems

Part One

"True poems flee."
            Emily Dickinson

Eventide

One of those evenings the dog slips its leash.
Tree branches scarring a yellow moon.
The saucy stars conspiring.

One of those evenings peace officers loathe.
The mad resigned to their fate.
A drunkard lost in his bedroom.
Civilization's smoke rising over the rooftops,
as if gravity had given up on us
and our slow blue world.

A page turns in a family bible.
In the harbour is a sloop named Solitude.
And the black bat, resuming its lifelong journey —
a traveler come to the country of night.
As if such things were worthy of a mention.

Of Course, This was Some Time Ago

There were two wrongs making a right,
which needn't concern us at this juncture.
Instead, consider my invisible master
pulling on an infinite number of trousers.
See the rat in the magical maze of my mind
mop his shining brow with his little rat-handkerchief
before bravely continuing a nearly impossible task.
Notice, if you would be so kind as to bother,
the eternal bickering between light and dark matter.
It's gotten so you don't know whether to spit or go blind.
These dusty old books of ours are so heavy and faded
we have to put on our spectacles and squint real hard.
And still we're not sure what it is that's running toward us.
Or is it, as someone suggested, we who are running away?

We Who Flee

A road, and little else.
No sky. No shapes. No planet.

A road linking two expectancies,
running between unfulfilled wishes,
going from exodus into exile,
from anywhere to somewhere other.

Behind us, a wash of memories
scented of almonds.
Behind us, a vague recollection.
A line being rubbed out.
A road sign in ancient Babylonian.

I applaud its unnamed makers.
I celebrate my ability to see
the sure logic of their sublime madness.

Getting There

Up ahead, a night without sleep.
Up ahead, a self-fulfilling prophecy,
which includes a mortician's off-key laughter
and full measure of the horsefly.

"We're on a road," I tell my shadow,
that laggard falling behind, the one trembling
at the thought of approaching night.

I peer from the runnels of my sadness . . .
Up ahead, a wedding cake on fire.
The undertaker, waving his black pamphlets.
A hill with a bloody gash in it.

"We're no farther along," I inform my angel.
She answers with an immense silence.
She winks. She beckons with a crooked finger.

Trip

A one-way ticket into the infinite.
The sound of feet shuffling
and clothes being removed,
X more shopping days
until the inevitable sad ending,
the last candle on the last cake
absolutely snuffed out, our game
called on account of darkness.

Eternity, somewhere over there, I think,
a quiet neighbourhood at dusk,
perpetual evening nibbling the drapes,
blurring our faces and hands.
A searchlight sweeping the perimeter.
Silence wedded to dread.

Small Town Blues

Here's a town where it's always night.
A little town filled with sleep,
with soft breathing and nightingales,
its petty thieves stealing forty winks.
Where mice and cats play cat-and-mouse,
a single sputtering streetlight
reflecting upon the sources of darkness.

Welcome to where the stars come out
after a spell of warm rain.
A place couched in coy phraseology.
A town without beginning or end.

Just the moon's face in a window.
A lone train whistle going unheard.
The last stop before morning.

Dark and Stormy Night

The meter is running,
rain scoring the wind,
coming down hard
on the town of New Apocalypse,
my cab driver smoking a cheroot,
smiling without smiling,
red-eyed, racing the lights,
with me slumped in the back seat
and as drunk as a lord.

Here! Stop here! I shout,
on a street among other streets,
the taxi easing to the curb,
the driver looking back in disbelief.
Seeing what little matters.

One Morning

The morning night ended.
The morning I lay in the bed's snow
making tight little angels,
clinging to the last starbeam,
considering seriously the nature of light,
of light's long and thankless journey
through the sovereign dark.

Morningtide, in bed with the blues
and a black cup of coffee,
gnawing a nail to the quick,
chewing on the straw of contemplation.
Thinking about daylight's simile.
Inventing, in the cold clean light of day,
a metaphor for invention.

Dragged Out in Chains

An utterly indifferent
morning in a world that
doesn't give a damn.
Not the crack of dawn,
but a fissure. Not
a sunrise, but a gate
in the earth, Father
Night slumped in his
chair, writing his
will, or a confession,
or a poem, first light
like a gun to his head.
Or God's finger. Or
a stick prodding.

This Too Passes

A time between time,
late summer evening, soil in decay,
the worm-fattened birds burning in the trees,
and all their songs about flying . . .

A portion of time so realized
it assumes breadth and magnitude,
the two of us caught up in it,
the momentous back currents,
the eddies of the self's oblivion
and soul's sweetened annihilation.

The actual second you said something
so profound it was impossible to comprehend.
Or I couldn't understand because I hadn't heard.
Or I'd heard, but I did not listen.

Haunted House

We go there to throw stones at ourselves.
We're sleeping, and dream we are there,
the house inside the house, night's headquarters.
Who knocks? The door is only implied.
Why enter? The rooms will come to you, in time.

The house behind a hill called Hell.
A little cry under its ethereal eaves,
apparitions steaming the windowpanes,
death's breath not what you'd call *enticing*.

Like smoke, I mow down a hallway.
Like fog, I embrace the chill measure
of a life lived after death-in-life.
An ether, I am wholly spiritual in nature.

One of the lost. One of the living.

Address Unknown

The mailman at the end of time . . .
On a flight of stairs
that never ends, that never begins.
On a street with a kink in its neck.
In a city whose name we've forgotten.

The mailman, our bewinged messenger,
sighing like a punished child,
fumbling in his bottomless mail sack,
plucking out the last dead letter.

That's him whistling past the graveyard,
squinting at the unearthly handwriting,
the usual elements plotting against him,
as they must do us all.
The boulevards, like twine, unwinding.

House to House

A salesman is going door to door.
He's selling bottled rain, sniffed fingers
and seraphim-scented handkerchiefs.
A salesman, in an ill-fitting suit,
is selling love-powder and paper aqualungs.
A mouse's shrugs. Dents in a bucket.
Bio-degradable emotion detectors.

The uninvited, leaning on your front door's bell,
hauling a scuffed satchel, carrying snake-hips
and vapourous handles. Hair dye for the dead.
A swastika of smoking ashes.

Who's selling two absolutes for a dollar,
the semi-divine, and storm windows too —
lest yon tempest offend thee.

Absentee Landlord

The house with bones on the lawn.
The house with the hidden basement,
its spooks stowed in the web-ridden attic.
Where the nervous newspaper boy
refuses to deliver and it's always dark,
windows dust-rimed and blacked-out,
the blinds drawn since Day One,
its flowerbeds filled with headless roses.

The house you rent by the minute,
its garden path cracked and gnarled,
its front door marked with a sign,
with, I suppose, the blood of a lamb.
And the only sound on the streets —
footsteps, fleeing in terror.

Moth to a Flame

It's only a mannequin in a storefront window.
It's just a display dummy, blissfully unaware,
an awkward smile on its perfected lips,
as patient as sin, waiting for its new suit
or the latest line in casual sports attire,
frozen with anticipation, dust gathering,
the morning light revealing little else
to the passerby or the kind-eyed wino
who's stopped to comb his flyblown hair
in the reflection from the plate glass window.
The very same man who returns after midnight,
the usually busy shopping precinct empty then,
the dummy *still* smiling, as if a joke being shared,
a little in-joke with its terrible punchline.

Glass and Steel

Some people work underground,
moving in and out of the Earth.
Some labour among air,
hanging from physics' invisible wires.
Others cross the waters,
carrying goods and restless humanity.

And then there's fire,
fire delivering us from night,
its heat, its alchemical purpose.
There are some who work with fire
and are never burned,
the arsonist envious of their medium,
their shop doors left open to the elements,
ajar to the constant bellows of winter.

Lost Ticket

The pawn shop at the edge of town.
A pawn shop in the City of Screams,
nothing in its window but flyspecks and webs
and a handful of time remaining.

A pawn shop loaning out midnight
and the musty quiet of tombs.
Where all that's unwanted goes.
Where dreams die and rainbows end.
And something else, too, you can't put your finger on.

Peering inside you see little on the shelves
but oaths being thoughtlessly broken,
a bit of used moonlight going cheap,
a last remnant resembling anything like human dignity.
And a few tattered memories. A few doleful laments.

Out of the Way Place

A little juke-joint in a forgotten borough.
Where the sunset goes at the end of a long day,
demented jazz playing into the demon-hours,
fallen angels serving us our black wine,
women with the heads of horses bringing us
dishes of meat, platters of sun-fattened strawberries,
moving with just a hint of what it is to be divine,
of what it means to be in the service of the infinite.

My fellow metaphysicians, enter, if you will,
a roadside inn outside of space and time,
discordant voices arguing in its back kitchen,
incense and perfume performing their heady dance,
the goat-footed proprietor counting souls like money.
Unashamed in his nakedness.

Gag Order

The last night on Earth
slipped quietly away.
The sky turned from that deep
rich blue the Sumerians so loved
to a godawful abyssal black.

Drinkers in the Sword and Rosary
paused between breaths
as an infinitely fabulous
maker willed them from one
level of existence to another.

Then somebody somewhere
said something bordering on wise –
as if anyone were listening.
And the less said about it the better.

Part Two

"Language is a virus from outer space."
William S. Burroughs

The Volume of Man

My body is filled with dovecotes and spoons.
I contain geraniums and warheads.
Sloshing about inside me are clouds and ditches.
There's peculiar scenery and savage imagery.
Instead of a heart, a Roman catapult.
Instead of lungs, galloping palominos.

There's a highway inside me that's going nowhere.
It's just below the surface, a sub-molecular reality,
and very earthy it is too, very meaty.
Often I walk this road alone,
cutting a forlorn figure, I imagine.

In a single sentence we approach ourselves.
We meet, exchange pleasantries, and are soon parted;
gladly relieved of our beautiful burden.

Whatever

Gifts of crickets and quicklime.
Gifts of camellias and tiger's wine.
Kohl, so you may outline your glance.
Lapis lazuli, for the skies in morning.

But isn't it hard on Earth?
Shouldn't we be more practical?
The flask of water for the long desert run.
A flint for fire-starting.
Butter and flour for our hunger.
Nothing superfluous. No luxury.
No baubles meant for idle hands or mind.

Even a palace intended for a demigod
requires a base and firm foundation.

Even a lightbeam is grounded in science.

Moving Target

I think you'll find I'm wearing a peanut costume.
I think you'll find me in the interstellar chicken coop.
That I'm the cloven-footed boy declaring himself to be Pan
or a dud bomb or I'm struggling with a flashlight.
I'm like a punch in the lamb or golf cart's battery.
I have charcoal incisors.

Stare, bloody ingrate, look hard and you'll see
a man with a mouthful of trash cans and trees.
You'll find me in the theatre of fits,
in the outhouse sewing bees, openly debating alien largesse.
As if a blind man who doesn't like what he sees,
you'll find I'm actually two princes buried under the stairs.
That I'm a misplaced government document.
A fractal in the cinema of the damned.

The Will of the People

You shouldn't play with fire, Mrs. River O'Blood.
Mr. Mind, refrain from toying with the sky's dominion.
Find a damp dark spot to sow your garden instead.
Build yourself a new house under a mossy stone.
It's beneath the earth that we set our finest temples.

Sister Digit, please, don't tamper with the light.
Quit breaking your million-and-a-half promises.
Our little mouse-ears are burning, our thoughts dulled.
The bugs inform us we are not immortal.

To the unborn I leave this iron begging-bowl.
I give up my bones to the seasons of high water.
It's a hard lesson I bestow upon my betters —
how their arrival denotes a sense of departure.

In a Bottle

A shithouse door flapping in the wind,
God's God sleeping in a burnt-out van,
the hurried messenger racing from Aix axed
for bold-faced belligerence in a theatre of war.
A slue of instances, and each unrelated,
tellingly obscure and yet somehow meaningful,
our best minds left gasping, gurning, guessing –
the usual who, what, when, where, why and how . . .

So you can stop mooning me with those big brown eyes;
all my answers are in the form of questions,
everything I know reduced to a note in a bottle.
Once tossed in the sea, it's now returning to shore.
And what blurred message awaits the reader?
A question in the form of an answer.

The Message and the Messenger

The Queen of Amnesia holding court —
or as much as anybody cares to remember.
Her consorts, Nausea and Insomnia,
forgetting their places, their manifest roles
in the overall state of affairs.

A storm-ridden night of the realm,
a horseman galloping past sleepy hamlets,
a dark horse on a darker highway,
its black rider with a face like hell,
a rich stink rising in the long hall,
courtesans vaguely recalling how
to curtsy or curry favour,
good King What's-his-nut scolding a page,
and, three times, the messenger knocking . . .

Black Light

The stars are watching—
bonfires of ancient light,
like taillights of those departing
for wider, brighter, more quiet ports.

With my cardboard telescope I see
flames hopping from god to god,
fiery rooms of a matchstick castle,
TV sets running all lifetime long.

We used to lie on the lawn
and count the wounds in night's side.
Was that the sign of the cross?
Was that a crack in light's heaven?

Where the dark pours through
and those drowned are lost always.

Mortal Midnight

The telescope salesman pitches woo
to the absolutes of solitude.
He doesn't dally with night
or the intangible darkness.
His comets are low-eyed and listless.
His planets are doorways into sorrow,
coppery lights bleeding through the good linen,
Time's ministrations failing us all badly.

Here's the poor sap going broke
by the deflected light of the half moon.
To whom the one-eyed astronomer
pays a very little and grudging respect.
Whole sections of the sky dimmed
where his stars have fallen.

One Night Among Many

The stars are very diffident tonight.
A soft rain falling on an eye.
The world rocking gently.

One hell of a song-and-dance,
the stars are being difficult tonight.
They glow like buttonholes in quicksilver,
bristle with cosmological distemper,
quake with exceptional charm.

But civilization! Its fashionable stain!
cries the bookseller, cries the butcher at market.
Cry they who would wake safely.

Bedtime in the garden of the purely sublime . . .
As if a rose's petals, I shut my mind.
I am indefinite morning.

Falling Star

Wind strolling through a blacked-out garden,
poplars fluttering like kitchen curtains,
midnight tripping over itself on the way to the can.
When the falling stars come a-calling,
noise evicted from its little black house,
the wisest among us tucked into bed.
When even the creatures of the night begin
to seriously question existence's validity,
beseeching a mute and four-legged god
who may or may not actually be there,
who may or may not be considering
the poor dumb creatures' silent prayers.
A god much like our god, O spark of divinity,
who does, and who doesn't, actually care.

High Mass

The gusts worry. The forests repent.
Leaves rustling bring to mind applause,
each a face in a green audience
or paper money being thrown in the air.
Deep in the woods it's always midnight,
stars triumphing over the heartless dark,
the trembling creatures covering their eyes
for fear their dreams might escape them.
And each in love with a minor horror.

The unrepentant trees attend to their high mass,
black lines scratched onto a blacker surface.
It's about this time the moon comes around,
like an old man looking for a slipper.
From a pool of cold water, the moon rises.

God's Button

Mademoiselle Moon, an umber thumbprint,
a thought suspended by a silver thread,
a slurred voice in the sub-arctic tundra.

This is the high window where her light appears,
a sugary light, like salt thrown over a shoulder,
like whitewash spilt or a bucket of cream
spoiled by roiling thunder.

All these bats and stars in our hair,
the moon a gateway, a watering eye,
a stone wheel in a windmill
burnishing celestial flour.

Foolish me, I meant to write 'flower'.
The moon is a bough in the night-orchard.
Once a month she blossoms into menses.

Hush

It took seven days to assemble this silence;
seven days of the sun and sunlight's tonnage.
Seven nights it took for the world to close its mouth,
to build these dark and mordant waters.

The quiet booms and is trapped in amber,
the Earth held in a terrible hand
once noted for its strength and beauty.
Which is stilled, which is finally still.

All week the auction's din, a *mal aria*
of factory-sound, of the human roaring;
all week an abominable noise
and uncurtailable crashing of comets.

Tears, like huge blows, rained down like hell.
And then, on the seventh day, we rested.

Your Prayers are Welcomed

I'm strictly fictional.
I'm not here. I'm not real.
You'd get more sense out of a talking hedge.

A stickman drawn by the visually impaired,
I live in a toy house in the window of a junk shop.
A reanimate golem weighing in
from Lands Unknown,
I'm all puff and bluster,
a character in a dime novel,
a god who requires your faith,
your dogged loyalty,
who asks you to be resolute in one thing only:
that you believe in me unquestioningly,
all existence being finally fatal.

Condemned

Heaven, long ago abandoned,
looking as forlorn as a derelict pier,
as quiet as daybreak after a heavy snowfall.
No one around, even the chubby cherubs fled,
bent haloes and wing-feathers scattered like litter
where the High and Mighty once stood –
or should I say *glimmered*?

Formerly Club Paradise, currently haunted
by the absence of any supernal presence,
those 'beatific' clouds now deflated and soiled,
a tangle of harp strings underfoot
and Mr. Big Shot nowhere to be seen,
the pearly gates not so inviting anymore,
their hinges squeaking in the once-scented wind.

The Infinite Voice-Over of Eternal Essences

We're taking you live to the holy Vatican,
its skull-and jewel-encrusted catacombs.

A door opens onto a bishop's water-closet.
Note the many hellish visions contained therein.

We bring you a cardinal's slippers,
satin brocade and velvet ribbons hand-stitched
by sinners beyond any hope of redemption.

Now to a close-up of St. Peter's bone.
In gold leaf. Etched with Latin.

To a long pan of the papal ring-finger,
that feels and smells like an actual soul,
El Papa himself absented from the scene.

But whose voice is that booming off-screen?
Our unearthly Master screaming in the rafters.

Unquenchable Fire

In hell, a crackpot socio-biologist.
An ex-monk, a pope, an emperor.
Your favourite stars from television.

Vast ranks sent to hell for sowing discord.
For lust, despair and profligacy.
For evil counsel. For wrath. For eonism.

In hell, a red wind and rain of hot rocks.
Demons raking blades through bowels.
Belial roasting infants' pinkies.
The lord of flies mounting his dung heap.

All attendant ceremonies presided over
by 'that most ancient friend of wisdom'.
The one who goes by many names
in the many hells of our own making.

Deep Blue Sea

Your devil sings to the fly in my soul.
Your devil invades the soul's moist clefts,
informing us with his pestilence,
the few good people gleaming in the hereafter,
the wicked in the throes of perpetual torment.

Your devil drinks liquid chlorine
and stripped the gears on my transmission.
He's soused on mothers' milk
and was found lifting a young nun's habit.
He brings to our table the gift of horsemeat.

That's his face clouding the window's glass.
That's his hand under the bedcovers,
his voice in your ear cooing, "I love you madly."

Mercilessly teasing the damned.

Part Three

"Everywhere I go I find a poet
has been there before me."
                    Sigmund Freud

Sonnet Despairing

Little animals immolated by Tragedy's fires.
Babies on pitchforks, War loading a haywain.
Death cutting Ma's throat in the kitchen.

We take you to a church in the countryside,
the vicar trembling, aching for a slug of wine,
a painting of the Madonna bleeding tears,
bullet holes where her eyes ought to be,
wee Jesus missing a few fingers.

We fly on broomsticks over the capitol,
dropping leaflet-bombs on the veterans' parade,
pissing down the Widow Forsythe's chimney,
cackling like hell, like the ill-fated mad.

Or worse, we don't do anything.
We stand aside. We let it all be.

It Is Our Nature

The magic in sorrow. The beautiful dead.
Putting love aside, like a favourite guitar,
after the wars of mind and body.

Life is without ease, without warning signs
or notice of deep water and dangerous undertow.
The soul is in question, murdered by Time.
The story of the flesh has its inescapable ending.

And still we ford a snow-fed river,
walking to the factory in a heavy rain,
pushing out the body, full bore under the challenge.
Going hard into the forests of the mind.
Trawling the good fathoms, as well as the bad.
Not forgetting death, but not remembering;
acceptance being in no way capitulation.

The Christmas Syndrome

It's always winter . . .
There's always snow falling
outside the women's penitentiary,
a north wind mugging snowdrifts,
icy blasts shaping beautiful patterns,
setting records for all-time lows
while the curious mind imagines
the feminine wiles
of such a captive audience,
ladies in restraints, their bare feet
crossing a cold stone floor.
One imagines midnight and weeping.
The steel door of a cell closing.
A name being softly spoken.

A Long Stretch in the Slammer

The abandoned penitentiary,
a place the crows avoid, a blot
on an otherwise enlightened century.

The crowbar hotel, ghosts of the guilty
arm-wrestling with their consciences,
vainly proclaiming innocence,
their cries like tin cups
dragged across iron bars,
each moment equivalent to an eternity.

The house of correction, time rolling
backwards down remorse's steep incline,
the cons returned to their darkened houses.

Souls weighed by a higher power.

Everlasting Pardon

A searing day and road gang in chains,
marching lockstep into the foreverness,
their manacles rattling in the annihilate,
a black sun bearing down hard,
not a breath or breeze in the mid-day heat,
the convicts building a road to nowhere,
a road over the deserts of the eternal,
the last hour on Earth beginning to end.

And their perpetually vigilant overseers,
grim-faced men glaring in the noon glint,
worse men perhaps than their prisoners —
a chain gang of rough-hewn criminals
in a place without pity.

Where the invisible abounds freely.

Zip Your Lip

Shut up! Shut up! Shut up!
I can't make this point too clearly.
Because your mouth is a chasm
and each sentence a rockslide.
Because your lips and tongue
are merely flapping in the wind.
Like a torn flag on a pole.
Like a bag in an updraft.

Stop talking and start walking.
Or at the very least say something
we might want to hear – like news
from home or the local ball scores.

You could catch flies with a mouth like that.

You could fit your entire fist in it.

It's a Living

Even Mr. Death takes a holiday.
A languid picnic in a minefield, a day trip
to Dachau, a non-stop tour of the killing fields.
The grim nature of his work aside,
he's much like us in many ways,
putting his trousers on one leg at a time,
fidgeting impatiently in long queues,
idly enquiring into the state of the weather.

Poor Mr. D, who has been working the night shift
longer than anyone cares to remember, and yet
is still amazed by mankind's cruelty and invention,
by their inability to grasp the gravity of the situation.

It's no surprise he throws himself into his work.

Small wonder he loses himself to the moment.

Cometh the Hour

Can't you sense it, son of a bitch?
Something is coming over the fields.
Something approaches us on its stomach.
Some say it's winter, or an army of snow.
Some suggest a muted messenger.
Everyone nods when death is mentioned.

It's marching out of the seventh level,
dragging a chain, a bad foot, a giant's head.
It flies out from the valleys of reason,
my sweetest demons prattling in their beds,
all my soft monsters despairing,
the sun blighted, the air scoured.

But it's only the rain, an optimist declares.
Schools darken, our churches condemned.
It's only the plague of our indifference.

Nowhere Now

Getting dressed is too much to ask.
Brushing my teeth will be the death of me.
By simply lifting this tumbler of water,
I'm put in mind of navies slipping beneath the sea.

I bring the water to my bruised lips.
I toast the dissemination of the senses.
I'm transported by undermen into Catatonia,
with its blue suns and sickly flowers.
A mood arrives in its torn black envelope,
the Ancient One stirring his pot of loins,
his cackle heard round the world, bones snapping,
a void in the coffee table opening.

And a man much like me, twitching like a nerve,
made miserable with want and winter.

A Solitary Mister

There's a letter in the mailbox.
A knock at the door.
The telephone is ringing.

All night long the people next door
could be heard to be breathing –
a ragged breath in, a fetid breath out.

While I dreamt of swarming crowds,
of their immolation amongst fiery furnishings.
I dreamt of bad sleep and stifled screams,
sirens tearing the sheets into strips,
choppers surveying the lawns,
shouts of the disenfranchised
scoring the urban blight . . .

All my life I have slept with the hunted.

The Bee's Knees

It's only suddenly dawned on me,
how I'm nothing more than sand in a shoe.
That I'm a puppet in a seaside skit.
A minor character in a beach novel.
How I resemble most a reflection
in a carnival's trick mirror.

And here I thought I was the pig's wings,
the caterpillar's kimono, the gnat's elbows.
Instead of this tongue-tied parrot I've become,
the one spouting self-righteous epithets in order
that he might confirm his paltry existence.

And not this monkey on a string.
Not this breeze over the city dump I am.
This creaking wheel. This lousy haircut.

Can You Spare an Emotion?

We were so poor we had to eat ourselves.
We wore patched and sad expressions.
The angels were evicted from our purses.

Back then, post-debacle,
home was a can by the side of the road.
We'd steal crumbs from the mice,
who'd only snatch them back again.
You were well off if you could afford to be lonely.

In those days we'd fight for breathing room.
We'd argue over scraps of wrapping paper.
We'd stoop as low as drinking another man's water.

Tough times, we couldn't spare an extra word.
Just a kid, I had to walk nine miles through snow
to get to a point in the far distance.

Chez André

Indulge! Minute steak from a previous century.
Pudding made from the language of men.
Boulders, gently sautéed in temporality.

Would you like a hair with your salad?
Do you care to nibble on the menu,
perhaps take a bite out of a spoon,
chew over some very personal decisions?

How about a nice slice of archangel pie
or stir-fried souls in gun-oil?
Perhaps the girl in the wheelchair prefers coffee?

Pouring over a wine list writ on water
is a drunken barber muttering "In a pig's eye."
His spectral waitress is hovering nearby.
Her lipstick is smeared. Her delicate slip is showing.

After a Long Night

The wind singing in the higher registers.
Steeplejacks reining in their lines.
Our minister clinging to his black hat.

It's the first day of winter, the masses
finding it difficult to temper undue suspicions,
their kind usually avoiding the likes of me,
the short and sweet and surly type,
a last sane peasant in the fiefdom of Glee.
Informal. Non-linear. Star-shaped in a round world.
The grump who relishes the idea of trees bowing
to chill gusts and the promise of a storm to come.
The one rehearsing lines from a play not yet written.
The sort who notices the wind and marks it down.
A very short book made of long sentences.

Charming

A book of spells, one for which
I've paid a hefty price, its pages
smeared with the blood of the
damned, stuck together with
the ancients' jism, passages
marked by a mysterious hand,
gobbledygook written in the
margins, what seems to be a
train of tears staining the aged
paper. Spells for lovers spurned,
for finding what is lost, and that
should probably remain so. And
a spell that doesn't do anything,
Lord, for which we are grateful.

In a Burning Book

I found myself lost
in the Forests of Night.
Each unsure step taken
was a word being erased.
My breaths hung like hoot owls
watching from the high branches.
My ragged blood
was the source of Sleep's river.

All night I wandered
in and out of the same mind,
a cut-out moon guiding the way,
like a maenad in a dark wood,
like Humbaba among the cedars,
and he imprisoned eternally by trees.

A Book

Is furniture in an abandoned house.
Hand-mirror to the thirteenth apostle.
A stone to weigh you down in bed.

A book is a path through the labyrinth,
a bomb for blowing up young minds,
a plough in a snowstorm.

It can be a prim garden
or nightmarish forest.
For some, it's an iceberg.
For others, a homely hearth,
bitter tincture, knowing mistress,
an infant in a fit of tears.

A book is a quiet room,
each page turned a door being opened.

Mouthful

Some words are bigger than others.
They take up more air, give us more lip,
use many more of the mouth's muscles.
They take longer to say, often unpronounceable,
with unexpected twists, hidden syllables,
extra letters tucked away in some darkened nook.
The type of word favoured in spelling bees,
the students stumbling over their tongues —
as if they've been given a trick question.

The kind of words rarely used, being difficult,
the foreign speaker wondering 'why and how',
my thesaurus baffled, the dictionary mum,
proving some things are better left unsaid,
how some truths are best unspoken.

Not That Poem

This poem is withdrawing from society.
This poem is lacking in sensibilities
usually shared with great literature,
that are thought common to poetry.
It's wallowing in self-denial.
It won't let you see it naked.

The parents of this poem are out on the tiles.
They've forgotten about their darling child,
its one hand splashing in gasoline
and the other reaching for the red button.

This poem is being abandoned
to the forces of a genuinely cruel nature.
'Mother' nature, some would call her.
The scarlet whore.

On Paper

There's a city inside my book,
graffiti, streetlights, horns honking.
On page nine is a line of houses.
In one paragraph a cistern overflows.
Behind a word two hoodlums lie in wait.

I roam the streets of my book,
peeking into lit-up windows,
chased away by a barking dog,
followed by a self-coined policeman —
unaware I'm the author of his existence.

There's a room in the city in my book,
away from the riotous mobs.
Where I must conclude my creations are mad.
Where I come to my own conclusions.

Squinting

Nearing the point of collapse,
and how little it seems likely
I shall ever write that one great poem.
Physically bankrupt and my mind dwindling,
the need for words lessens,
so only a glad silence
will emanate from my throat,
a spare delight in my savage artistry,
the soul out wandering,
admiring the view
and the soul's reflections,
each poem or song a vanity mirror,
each poem and song a broken lens
of my fantastic glasses.

Posthumous Opus

After you die the earth reconsiders
your mass and earthly dimensions.
An unseen hand builds an unseen house.
Your blood goes to sleep for a very long time,
relatives arguing over gewgaws and furniture.
Your death is interpreted by seers.
Immediately your dog becomes despondent.
Ghosts gamble at dice for your clothes.
A small flame surfaces from underground.
An odd sort of wind comes along
and covers your name in handmade satin roses.

After you die all that *is* carries on,
much as it always had before.

The world exists without you.

Part Four

"Poetry is an orphan of silence."
                    Charles Simic

Love Is Also a Weapon

The journey from light into shadow.
The left hand sullying the right.
A nod and a wink toward self-destruction.

They blame the god or the gun.
Weakened, lured by a familiar scent,
they fall under the bulls' hooves.

Brethren, that's not The Hag hovering overhead,
it's the lifelong conflict of body and soul —
this is what started the famines and fires.
This is the cot for birthing warfare.

Demons smaller than bacterium
are running their hands over our daughters.
The eventual worm is consuming the rose.
It's devouring the last of beauty.

Trial by Fire

My girl is a fallen angel,
her voice like a ball gown being unzipped,
her eyes dust devils in the spiraling distance.
With a mouth that's a rose, thorns and all.
And what legs! As if a pathway into heaven.

Fellas, I admit it, I'm wild about her,
my perfumed summer breeze,
my little sweet-assed petunia,
my darling love-rocket.

Which is why I'm intensely jealous.
I wouldn't want to lose a drop of her blood.
I'm loathe to have to beat her with love's stick.
I'd really hate myself
if anything awful were to happen.

A Seven-Headed Love Story

I love your ankles, Mrs. Anderson.
Your underwear drawer. The pins in your hair.
Mrs. Anderson, I love your dishwater.
You've a wholesome bosom.

Missus, our star signs were destined for one another.
Our exhaled carbon molecules co-mingle.
Our scars match. We even smell like each other,
our thoughts coming together, but our lives apart.

It's about your husband, Mrs. Anderson.
The water on his brain. That unavoidable accident.
My imperfect pearl, it's about your children,
none of whom shall ever bear my name,
my pain, my martyred flesh,
my blushing genes in the mansions of pride.

Cold Flame

I'm coming home to be with you.
After the blizzard of the bottle
and waist-deep in black snow.
Post traumatic stress syndrome.
Much later than death first expected.

A pin, I wrestle with a needle.
I've carved your initials
into the tree of my arm.
Our photons are jangling
like cheap costume jewelry
during heartache's Mardi Gras.
We lie beside tumultuous rivers.

Here, sip this sweet illusion.
My beautiful outcast, drink of me.

Assigned False Planets

A paper wing and barbed-wire halo.
A sword made of charitable acts.
The good book of demons and a bomb's wit.

It was the morning the altar boy went mad,
the very day the war of the angels ended.
We were being good by being bad,
in the same way light leads into darkness.
Someone had put salt in all the sugar bowls.
They'd just proven non-existence existed,
the newspapers buzzing with neuroses.
Networks filmed their own eventual demise.
A wolf sued a lamb for non-compliance.
The rabid fox of intuition
raided the henhouses of reason.

Beautiful Monster

I'm building the beautiful monster.
Wishes and prayers are my raw materials.
With a pinch of irony and strained emotions.
And now adding a dash of bitterness.

This is my monster on a streetcorner.
That smells of labour's perspiration.
A creature with teeth like paving slabs.
Its breaths thickened with regret.
A storm in the night for its consciousness.

Alive, my monster is like a northern forest,
every thought a snow-laden pine branch.

We polish a claw together.
Twins, we recoil in wonder.

We carry one another.

The Play of Shadows

Shadows are all that we have left
after a long telephone conversation.
Shadows are other people, but in retrospect.

Today, my shadow ran on ahead,
its mouth bloodied from an iron bit,
frothing like a maddened stallion —
and yet as curious as a puppy.
Tonight, it's a melody worming in my head
or a dream-door slamming in the pantry.
It's all these words my left hand has written.

Oh shadow, evicted from the House of Fun.
Dear shadow, your chuckles like a pulley creaking
or bottled-up emotion or dog's squeaky toy.
The fifth of nine essences.

Mystery Play

All the lost children
in the singular forest.
Their cries at twilight.
The threads of their tears.

Snowfall at nightfall . . .
In a suburb of dark mansions
are their toy-cold engines.
This must be Christmas,
and here is a child's sleigh,
a few bird-souls in the bent branches
calling and calling — unfound prayers
of an old religion, the last word
of the last song salting a cut lip.

The tragedy of non-existence.

First Night

A play, showing in the theatre
of dreams, based on your journal
of thoughts scribbled in a bombed-out
basement during a somewhat lengthy
incarceration. Suddenly, stormtroopers.
Discordant music from the orchestra
pit as the set collapses, the scenery in
flames, your play, it seems, a musical
now, a timely warning, a pantomime,
the leading lady foolishly whistling
in her dressing room, her long sulk
bringing the house down, the lead
in her pancake make-up working
its inexorable way under the skin.

My Life in Movies

I stood at the corners
of Nothing and Nowhere streets,
a cigarette dangling from my pouting lips.
I forewarned Time and Beingness —
you'd better beware,
flicking my switchblade menacingly,
greasing a comb through my hair,
waiting to be discovered.

That's me, right around midnight,
chewing on the toothpick of a thought,
trying hard to look and act hard
for the benefit of the cameras;
the ones I imagine following me
down this incredibly dark alley.

Now Showing

A movie I'm not meant to understand.
A silent film, but in a foreign language,
its sub-titles melted as if in a downpour,
the sole noise an antiquated projector,
with only myself in this empty cinema,
a cold hand in the buttery popcorn
and a sense that I might be missing something,
something important, though I'll be stuffed
if I can tell you what it is at the moment.

On the mercurial screen ghostly figures
go about the business of fading from memory.
The fire curtain flutters purposelessly,
or at least not for any reason I can think of,
and the critics be damned . . .

Pratfalls and Slapstick

Nightfall at the Clown Academy,
mice arriving for their evening classes,
the instructors washing the chalk dust out
of their unreasonably unruly hair,
the dorms unsettling in their quiet.

It's so still you can hear the warm breezes
stalking the bushes on the quad,
the last junebug making its bed to lie in it.
You can listen to the grass thinking.

And the sad-eyed janitor in baggy pants,
the squeak in his shoe echoing
along the darkening corridors;
who's sweeping up the greasepaint tears,
the glittery residue of sorrow.

The Joke's on You

All attempts at humour have failed.
You can't be funny, not in poems,
not in school or church or prison;
where baring the teeth is a sign
of either aggression or instability.

The other day we were watching television.
A courtroom drama, the prosecutor punned,
some lame joke about horses and whores.
Well, talk about a hung jury . . .

Joviality, a symptom of weakness,
individuals putting their lives on the line
for a snigger or grin or guffaw.
Really, people, the bombs are dropping.
It's time to get serious. Very. Serious.

Wolf Song

The wolf in a field of maize.
A wolf in a grass circle.
In forests dividing morning from night,
a shadow among other shadows.

The gentleman-wolf in a business suit,
leaving a calling card on the wild boar's path,
a lamb's head in his leather valise,
and with a grin wider than any of the four seasons.

Ladies and gentlemen, introducing the wolf,
possessed of *unpresupposing* charm,
whose voice is the young doe's lullaby,
whose love is the final flower;
the wildflower, older than princes and war
and plucked from the white steppes mid-winter.

Bugged-Out

Insects in drawers, in display cabinets.
Bugs stuck to the stilts of silver stick-pins,
their compound eyes seeing what's unseen,
victims of their own success, Jurassic
survivors at odds with the vicissitudes
of Man, unreasonable mankind's gases
and oils mocking a Creator's favourites,
which He, in His all-knowing beneficence,
sprinkled far and wide over the countryside,
the bugs outnumbering sand grains and stars,
slaughtered for their itches, bites and stings,
butchered for their crawling and buzzing,
for going on six legs or eight legs or more,.
For daring to challenge our existence.

The Spider Says

I'm familiar with apprehension,
aware of doubt, sympathetic to terror.
Consider me a patient knot in a thread,
a little stone calling to the dark of the world,
the multi-eyed beast in her sullen quarter;
she who is tethered to a latch or a hair.

The spider says Sweet fly, sweetmeat,
think me the wraith to your gummy end,
my door invitingly ajar, the table always set.
And these are my babies, my thousands,
so curious, so ravenous, nimble copies
of copies, sentient pebbles fleeing hunger's edge.
It is they, era-perfect, who scurry.
I set them loose upon the edible earth.

Faint Olympian

The moth rattles like dinnerware.
A little book, she sputters awkwardly.
Dressed in night and powder
she turns to a mirror of flame,
seeing herself to be more beautiful
than ever we could imagine.

It's from a town of broken promises
that the moth begins her long journey.
In the chill dark the coy old girl
overcomes her flittering solitude.
A lamp coins its spell.
A struck match is a cosmos
being born out of nothing.
Unliving. Undying. Undead.

Death of a Mouse

Which is no great thing,
coming in from the frost-bitten fields,
meeting its mousey maker,
eternity's go-between the simple housecat,
a fat and playful agent of death.

The late mouse, its life poured out
on a mat by a door,
the watch of its heart stopped,
the wheel in its head no longer turning.

As must we all lie down,
a little dirt-nap for the fallen just,
an old wind aching in the yellowing glade,
fields of gold calling us home,
the grains of harvest piled high.

Under the World

Contemplate the root,
its gritty finesse,
its determined fingers
parting dirt from dirt.

Thirteenth house in a zodiac,
the root hangs on tightly
to the spin in the Earth.
The sixth book of seven,
the root is pure desire
churning reward from decay.

What reaches deep
into the global psalm?
A tender anchor
in the garden's acre.

Invention

Stick: the wrong end of.
For beating your belligerent mule.
The dog's stick, covered in drool.
That we whittled for the sake of whittling.

The stick that was matched to a stone,
and that broke my bones.
Carved as a cane and gone on a long journey.
The tallyman's stick,
each notch an item of cargo
or phase of the moon.

The last and first of sticks in a house of sticks,
pigs squealing their little pig-squeals
and the bad wolf over-excited –
breathless, but delighted.

Ponderous Breezes

Here's the bargain-basement philosopher
contemplating the red of a rose,
nature adding perfection to perfection,
language a mirror reflecting the mind,
one truth as viable as any other.

Presenting the cut-price metaphysician,
stinking of sophistry and aphorisms.
his every breath like Dr. Death
humming a jingle once heard on the radio.

Ideas trail behind him, build pyramids,
construct polyhedrons, discuss God's existence.
And that's the problem with philosophy —
Truth may, and it may not, be proven.
Not with words, with the bewitchment of words.

N Equals N

According to the emperor's new
physics zero possibly doesn't
exist and God may or may not be
reduced to a short-lived particle.

A thing is, and a thing isn't.
Very real. And completely fabricated.

On the blackboard is a formula
only the devil might solve –
he who resides beneath a decimal.
And the physicist, naked as a bone,
rubbing his imponderable chin,
tapping a mental pencil
against his graying temple –
because X matters.

Zero Point Zero

What equals what?
Nothing . . .
If you have five screams
and I take away nine?
Nothing . . .
What's left of the light?
More and more nothing.

Equivalent to Martian canals.
A measure of an atom's breadth.
The entire heft
of our valiant sleeping.

And that thing
at the height of things?
Pure nothing.

Here Is Now

A moment between moments.
The circle of instances,
where time begins and space ends,
this world finished
and another inventing itself —
"Out of nothing," you said,
a voice spoken at twilight,
nothingness like a small room
at the back of my head,
a dark room, the house empty . . .
"Just the occasional ghost," you said,
stirring your cup of Now,
the sound of breaths on the landing,
too slight to declare.

About the Author

Originally from Niagara Falls, Canadian-born Bruce McRae is a musician who has spent much of his life in London and British Columbia. Published in hundreds of periodicals and anthologies, his first book, 'The So-Called Sonnets' is available from the Silenced Press website or via Amazon books

CPSIA information can be obtained
at www.ICGtesting.com
Printed in the USA
LVOW04s0613281115
464483LV00032B/380/P